Hot Math Topics

Problem Solving, Communication, and Reasoning

Money and Time

Carole Greenes
Linda Schulman Dacey
Rika Spungin

Dale Seymour Publications®
Parsippany, New Jersey

Dale Seymour Publications
An imprint of Pearson Learning
299 Jefferson Road; P.O. Box 480
Parsippany, New Jersey 07054-0480
www.pearsonlearning.com
Customer Service: 800-321-3106

Editorial Manager: Carolyn Coyle
Project Editor: Mali Apple
Production/Manufacturing Director: Janet Yearian
Production/Manufacturing Manager: Karen Edmonds
Production/Manufacturing Coordinator: Roxanne Knoll
Art Director: Jim O'Shea
Text and Cover Design: Tracey Munz
Cover and Interior Illustrations: Jared Lee
Computer Graphics: Alan Noyes

ISBN 0-7690-0834-8

1 2 3 4 5 6 7 8 9 10-ML-04 03 02 01 00

This Book Is Printed On Recycled Paper

Contents

1 Ticket for $1.50
10 Tickets for $12.00
Dolphin Show:
8 A.M. and 1 P.M.
4 Tickets
Magic Show:
10 A.M. and 3 P.M.
3 Tickets

Introduction

Why Was *Hot Math Topics* Developed?

The *Hot Math Topics* series was developed for several reasons:

- to offer students practice and maintenance of previously learned skills and concepts
- to enhance problem solving and mathematical reasoning abilities
- to build literacy skills
- to nurture collaborative learning behaviors

Practicing and maintaining concepts and skills

Although textbooks and core curriculum materials do treat the topics explored in this series, their treatment is often limited by the lesson format and the page size. As a consequence, there are often not enough opportunities for students to practice newly acquired concepts and skills related to the topics, or to connect the topics to other content areas. *Hot Math Topics* provides the necessary practice and mathematical connections.

Similarly, core instructional programs often do not do a very good job of helping students maintain their skills. Although textbooks do include reviews of previously learned material, they are frequently limited to sidebars or boxed-off areas on one or two pages in each chapter, with four or five exercises in each box. Each set of problems is intended only as a sampling of previously taught topics, rather than as a complete review. In the selection and placement of the review exercises, little or no attention is given to levels of complexity of the problems. By contrast, *Hot Math Topics* targets specific topics and gives students more experience with concepts and skills related to them. The problems are sequenced by difficulty, allowing students to hone their skills. And, because they are not tied to specific lessons, the problems can be used at any time.

Enhancing problem solving and mathematical reasoning abilities

Hot Math Topics presents students with situations in which they may use a variety of problem solving strategies, including

- designing and conducting experiments to generate or collect data
- guessing, checking, and revising guesses
- organizing data in lists or tables in order to identify patterns and relationships
- choosing appropriate computational algorithms and deciding on a sequence of computations
- using inverse operations in "work backward" solution paths

For their solutions, students are also required to bring to bear various methods of reasoning, including

- deductive reasoning
- inductive reasoning
- proportional reasoning

For example, to solve clue-type problems, students must reason deductively and make inferences about mathematical relationships in order to generate candidates for the solutions and to hone in on those that meet all of the problem's conditions.

To identify and continue a pattern and then write a rule for finding the next term in that pattern, students must reason inductively.

To make trades and compute unit prices, students must reason proportionally.

To estimate or compare magnitudes of numbers, or to determine the type of number appropriate for a given situation, students must apply their number sense skills.

Building communication and literacy skills

Hot Math Topics offers students opportunities to write and talk about mathematical ideas. For many problems, students must describe their solution paths, justify their solutions, give their opinions, or write or tell stories.

Some problems have multiple solution methods. With these problems, students may have to compare their methods with those of their peers and talk about how their approaches are alike and different.

Other problems have multiple solutions, requiring students to confer to be sure they have found all possible answers.

Nurturing collaborative learning behaviors

Several of the problems can be solved by students working together. Some are designed specifically as partner problems. By working collaboratively, students can develop expertise in posing questions that call for clarification or verification, brainstorming solution strategies, and following another person's line of reasoning.

What Is in *Money and Time*?

This book contains 100 problems and tasks that focus on money and time. The mathematics content, the mathematical connections, the problem solving strategies, and the communication skills that are emphasized are described below.

Mathematics content

Money problems and tasks require students to

- identify and compare values of sets of coins
- generate sets of coins for specified amounts of money
- compute with amounts of money in dollars and cents
- compute unit costs or estimate to find the better buy

Time problems and tasks require students to

- estimate and compute elapsed time
- match events to amounts of time
- compare units for measuring time and convert between units
- interpret calendars and identify patterns on calendars
- order events temporally
- interpret and create schedules

Mathematical connections

In these problems and tasks, connections are made to these other topic areas:

- arithmetic
- algebra
- geometry
- graphs
- measurement
- statistics

Problem solving strategies

Money and Time problems and tasks offer students opportunities to use one or more of several problem solving strategies.

- **Formulate Questions:** When data are presented in displays or text form, students must pose one or more questions that can be answered using the given data.
- **Complete Stories:** When confronted with an incomplete story, students must supply the missing information and then check that the story makes sense.
- **Organize Information:** To ensure that several solution candidates for a problem are considered, students may have to organize information by drawing a picture, making a list, or constructing a chart.
- **Guess, Check, and Revise:** In some problems, students have to identify or generate candidates for the solution and then check whether those candidates match the conditions of the problem. If the conditions are not satisfied, other possible solutions must be generated and verified.
- **Identify and Continue Patterns:** To identify the next term or terms in a sequence, students have to recognize the relationship between successive terms and then generalize that relationship.
- **Use Logic:** Students have to reason deductively, from clues, to make inferences about the solution to a problem. They have to reason inductively to continue numeric patterns.
- **Work Backward:** In some problems, students have to work from what is known and apply inverse operations in order to determine what is not known.

Communication skills

Problems and tasks in *Money and Time* are designed to stimulate communication. As part of the solution process, students may have to

- describe their thinking steps
- describe patterns
- find alternate solution methods and solution paths
- identify other possible answers
- formulate problems for classmates to solve
- compare solutions and methods with classmates

These communication skills are enhanced when students interact with one another and with the teacher. By communicating both orally and in writing, students develop their understanding and use of the language of mathematics.

How Can *Hot Math Topics* Be Used?

The problems may be used as practice of newly learned concepts and skills, as maintenance of previously learned ideas, and as enrichment experiences for early finishers or more advanced students.

They may be used in class or assigned for homework. If used during class, they may be selected to complement lessons dealing with a specific topic or assigned every week as a means of keeping skills alive and well. Because the problems often require the application of various problem solving strategies and reasoning methods, they may also form the basis of whole-class lessons whose goals are to develop expertise with specific problem solving strategies or methods.

The problems, which are sequenced from least to most difficult, may be used by students working in pairs or on their own. The selection of problems may be made by the teacher or the students based on their needs or interests. If the plan is for students to choose problems, you may wish to copy individual problems onto card stock and laminate them, and establish a problem card file.

To facilitate record keeping, a Management Chart is provided on page 6. The chart can be duplicated so that there is one for each student. As a problem is completed, the space corresponding to that problem's number may be shaded. An Award Certificate is included on page 6 as well.

How Can Student Performance Be Assessed?

Money and Time problems and tasks provide you with opportunities to assess students'

- knowledge of time and money
- mathematical reasoning methods
- problem solving abilities
- communication skills

Observations

Keeping anecdotal records helps you to remember important information you gain as you observe students at work. To make observations more manageable, limit each observation to a group of from four to six students or to one of the areas noted above. You may find that using index cards facilitates the recording process.

Discussions

Many of the *Money and Time* problems and tasks allow for multiple answers or may be solved in a variety of ways. This built-in richness motivates students to discuss their work with one another. Small groups or class discussions are appropriate. As students share their approaches to the problems, you will gain additional insights into their content knowledge, mathematical reasoning, and communication abilities.

Scoring responses

You may wish to holistically score students' responses to the problems and tasks. The simple scoring rubric below uses three levels: high, medium, and low.

Portfolios

Having students store their responses to the problems in *Hot Math Topics* portfolios allows them to see improvement in their work over time. You may want to have them choose examples of their best responses for inclusion in their permanent portfolios, accompanied by explanations as to why each was chosen.

High	Medium	Low
• Solution demonstrates that the student knows the concepts and skills. • Solution is complete and thorough. • Student communicates effectively.	• Solution demonstrates that the student has some knowledge of the concepts and skills. • Solution is complete. • Student communicates somewhat clearly.	• Solution shows that the student has little or no grasp of the concepts and skills. • Solution is incomplete or contains major errors. • Student does not communicate effectively.

Students and the assessment process

Involving students in the assessment process is central to the development of their abilities to reflect on their own work, to understand the assessment standards to which they are held accountable, and to take ownership for their own learning. Young children may find the reflective process difficult, but with your coaching, they can develop such skills.

Discussion may be needed to help students better understand your standards for performance. Ask students such questions as, "What does it mean to communicate *clearly*?" "What is a *complete* response?" Some students may want to use the high-medium-low rubric to score their responses.

Participation in peer-assessment tasks will also help students to better understand the performance standards. In pairs or small groups, students can review each other's responses and offer feedback. Opportunities to revise work may then be given.

What Additional Materials Are Needed?

Real or play money, calendars, and calculators are required for solving some of the problems in *Money and Time*. Clocks may also be helpful.

Management Chart

Name ______________________

When a problem or task is completed, shade the box with that number.

1	2	3	4	5	6	7	8	9	10
11	12	13	14	15	16	17	18	19	20
21	22	23	24	25	26	27	28	29	30
31	32	33	34	35	36	37	38	39	40
41	42	43	44	45	46	47	48	49	50
51	52	53	54	55	56	57	58	59	60
61	62	63	64	65	66	67	68	69	70
71	72	73	74	75	76	77	78	79	80
81	82	83	84	85	86	87	88	89	90
91	92	93	94	95	96	97	98	99	100

Award Certificate

this certifies that

____

has been awarded the Hot Math Topics Super Solver Certificate for

Excellence in Problem Solving

______________________ ______________________

date signature

Problems and Tasks

1

Which movie is longer?

How many minutes longer?

Tell how you decided.

2

The movie was over at 3:00 in the afternoon.

What time did it start?

Tell who has which set of coins. 3

- Tess and Will have the same number of coins.
- Together, Kai and Tess have more than 30¢.

Write the names under the coins.

________ ________ ________

Renee bought 2 of these items. 4

What did she buy?

- She spent less than $20.
- She spent more than $10.
- She did not buy the baseball bat.

Renee bought the __________ **and the** __________.

Write a story problem using at least two of the times shown on the clocks.

Give your problem to a friend to solve.

On the 20th day of a month in 1969, people landed on the moon for the first time.

Use the clues to find the month.

Clues

- The month does not begin with *A*.
- The month has 31 days.
- The month does not have *R* in its name.
- The month is not in the spring.

I have 4 quarters, 3 dimes, 2 nickels, and 1 penny in my piggy bank.

If I shake out 4 coins, what is the least amount of money I will get?

8

How much does each toy cost?

- The boat and train together cost more than $30.
- The train costs $3 more than the boat.

The boat costs ______.

The train costs ______.

The car costs ______.

Toy Prices

9

There are apples, raisins, nuts, and juice for sale.

Write the price of each item.

- The nuts cost 2¢ less than half of a dollar.
- The raisins cost 10¢ more than a quarter.
- An apple costs 5¢ less than the raisins.
- An apple and juice together cost 69¢.

Draw the calendar page for next month.

Write the name of the month at the top.

Mark special dates on the calendar month.

Tell what you will do on those special days.

© Dale Seymour Publications®

12

The concert starts at 1:15.

The concert is 98 minutes long.

At what time will the concert be over?

List your thinking steps.

13

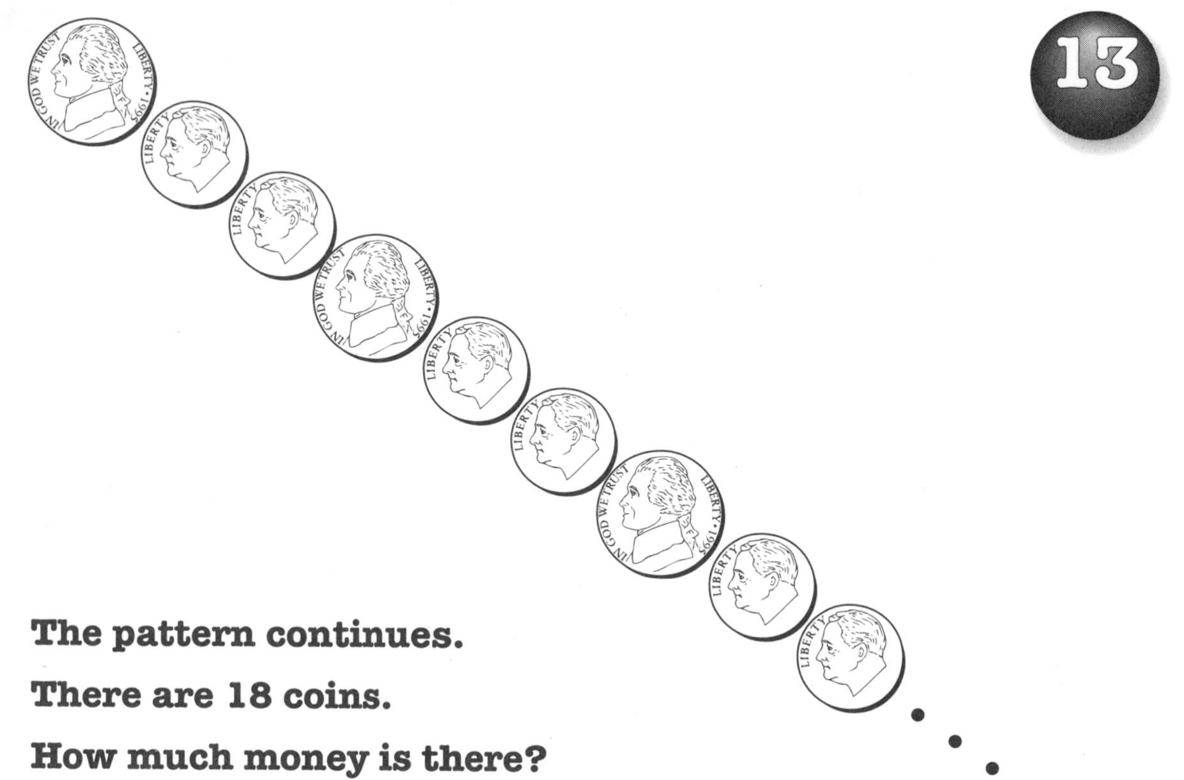

The pattern continues.

There are 18 coins.

How much money is there?

14

Jesse has this money:

Jesse went shopping.

Write a math problem about Jesse's shopping trip.

Have a friend solve your problem.

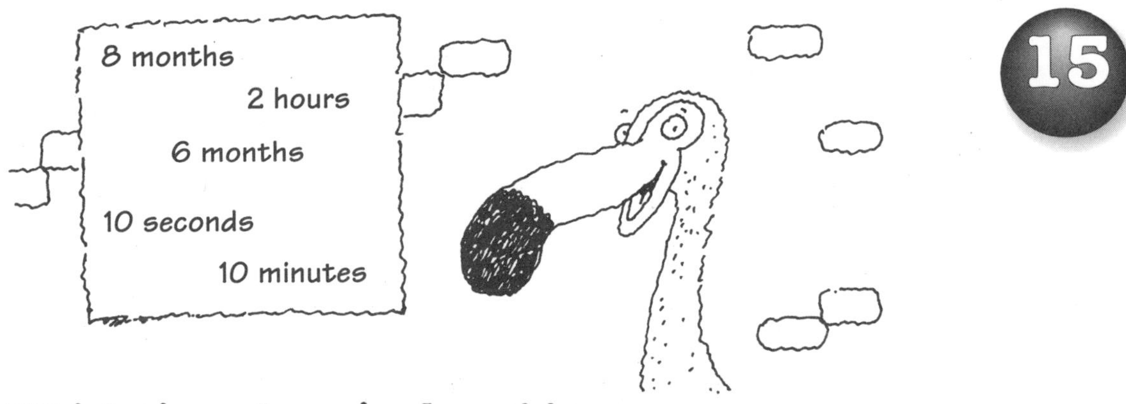

15

Which time above is closest to

- the time it takes to say the months of the year? __________
- the time it takes to play a basketball game? __________
- the time from Valentine's Day to Halloween? __________

Make up three more questions about these times.

Trade questions with a friend.

16

The school play, the school concert, and the school field day are on October 17, February 10, and March 25.

- The concert is not 4 days before Valentine's Day.
- The play is not 2 weeks before Halloween.
- The field day is 7 days before April Fool's Day.

Tell the date of each activity.

The play is on ______________.

The concert is on ______________.

The field day is on ______________.

There are 9 coins in the duck bank.

At least 2 of the coins are dimes.

The coins are worth 62¢.

How many dimes are in the duck bank?

Tell how you know.

18

PIZZA SHOP HOURS

Monday through Friday:
10 A.M. to 9 P.M.

Saturday:
11 A.M. to 11 P.M.

Closed Sunday

How many hours is the pizza shop open each week?

19

Write a price for each ride.

- The pony ride costs 50¢ more than the Ferris wheel.
- The water slide is the most expensive ride.
- The whirlybird costs 75¢ less than the bumper cars.
- The crazy cups are the least expensive ride.

20

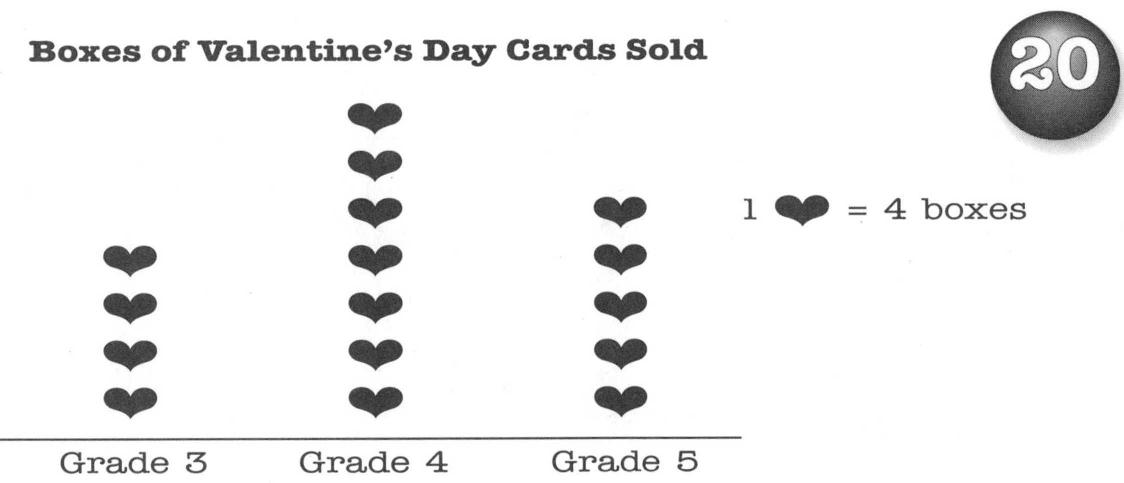

The students sold cards for $2.00 a box.

How much more money did the grade 4 students collect than the grade 3 students?

Tell how you know.

21

I have

- more than $5.50
- less than $7.00
- 1 bill
- 3 coins, all the same
- no quarters

How much money do I have?

How did you decide?

22

Fill in the blanks.

The story must make sense.

Shawna bought ______ yards of cloth for $______ per yard.

The total cost for the cloth was $______.

She gave the clerk a $10 bill and got back $______.

Compare your story with a friend's story.

23

I have $1.38 in coins.

What is the fewest number of coins I could have?

What are the coins?

What is the greatest number of coins I could have?

What are the coins?

The bar graph shows how many quarters each student has.

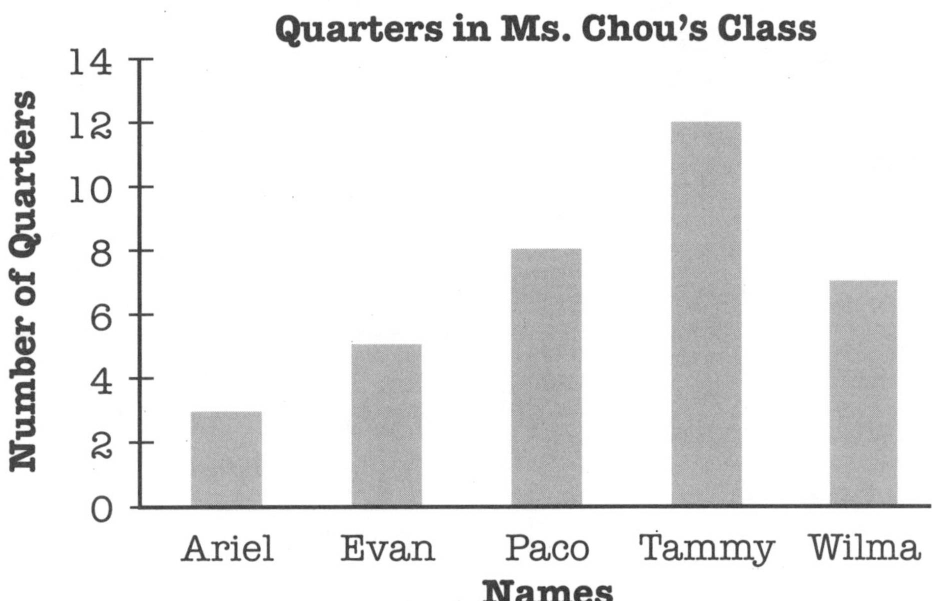

How much more money does Tammy have than Evan?

Tell two ways to decide.

Hani put his coins in 7 rows.

- The top and bottom rows each have just 4 quarters.
- The middle row has just 6 dimes.
- The other rows each have just 5 nickels.

What is the total value of Hani's coins?

26

How much more is the toll from Beakville to Flamingo Hill than the toll from Beakville to Wing City?

Toll Road Ticket	
Toll Charges from Beakville	
Route 2	$.15
Wing City	$.35
Birdtown	$.60
Route 190	$1.20
Flamingo Hill	$1.60

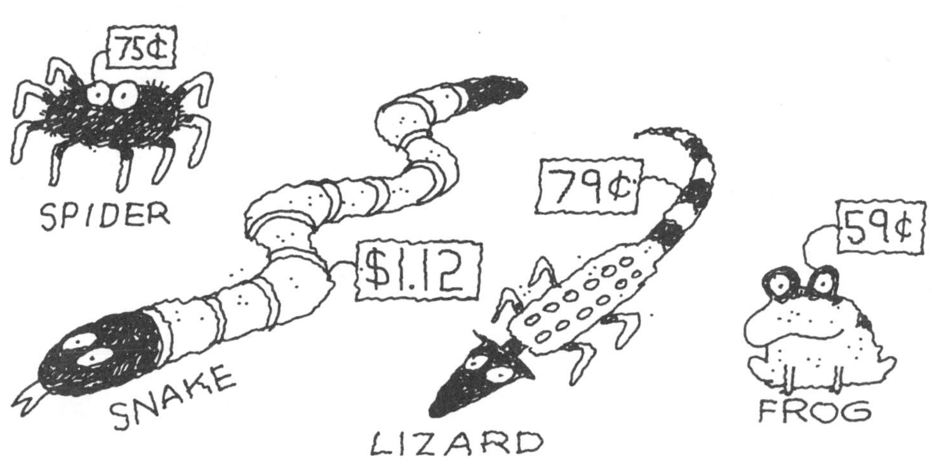

Emma has $3.30.

Does she have enough money to buy all 4 toys?

Tell how you can use estimation to answer the question.

Ms. Chow's bakery bill was $9.64.

- She gave the clerk a $10 bill.
- She got her change in the fewest number of coins.

What coins did she get?

GIANT END-OF-YEAR SALE!

29

Lou bought a belt and a pair of jeans.

Kamil bought a tie and a shirt.

How much more did Lou spend than Kamil?

30

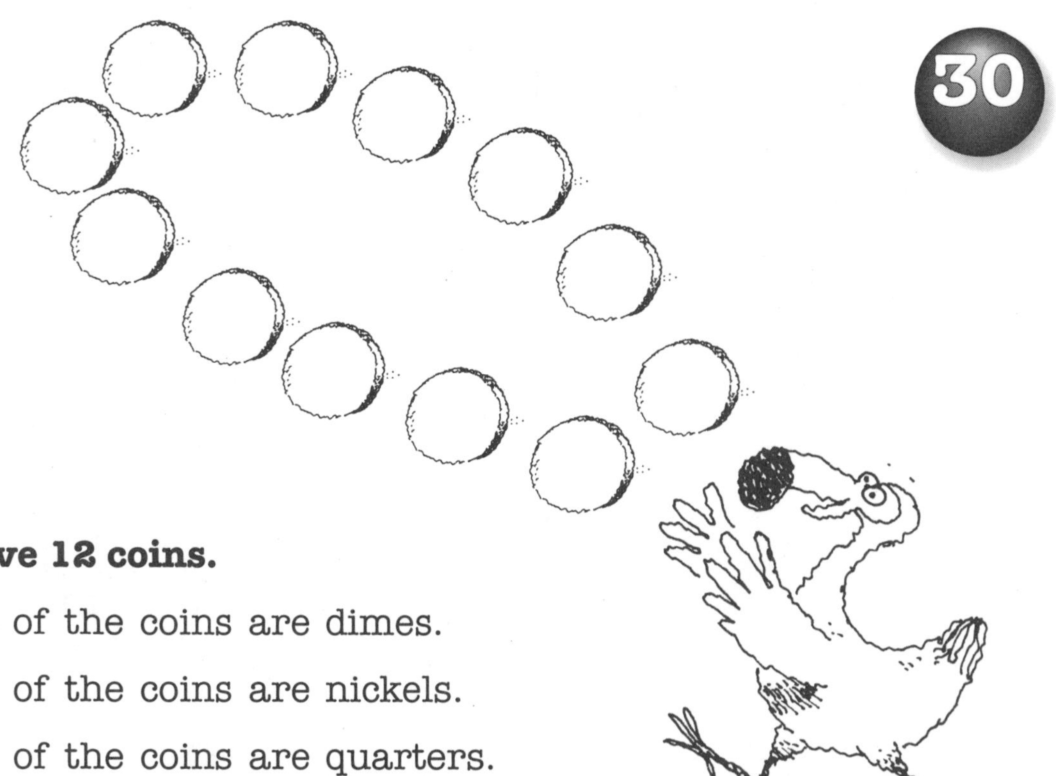

I have 12 coins.

- $\frac{1}{2}$ of the coins are dimes.
- $\frac{1}{3}$ of the coins are nickels.
- $\frac{1}{6}$ of the coins are quarters.

How much money do I have?

31

Lydia practices guitar on Monday, Wednesday, and Friday.

She practices from 3:30 until 6:00.

How many hours does she practice each week?

What time did Kim go to bed?

Rosa went shopping.

Rosa has $3.20 left.

How much money did she have when she started shopping?

How much was the salad?

How did you decide?

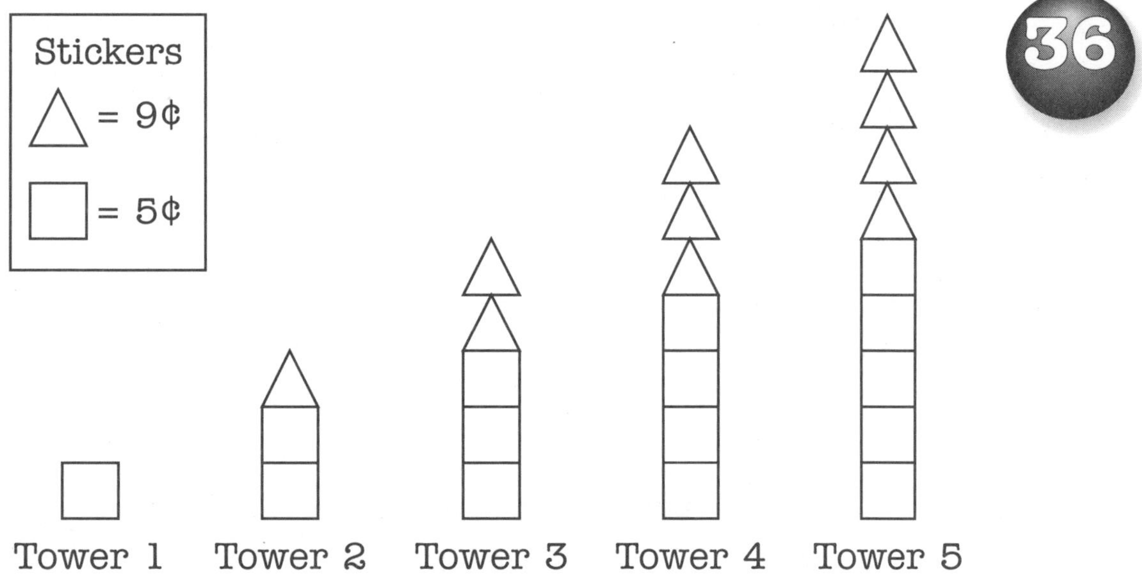

© Dale Seymour Publications®

The sticker pattern continues.

How much is tower 10 worth?

Which is more:

a dime for each week of the year

or

a nickel for each year of the century?

How do you know?

Fill each blank with a number from the bell.

The story must make sense.

In the year ______, the Liberty Bell in Philadelphia will celebrate its ______ th birthday.

The bell was given to Philadelphia in ______.

In ______, the bell was rung for the first reading of the Declaration of Independence.

January 2006

S	M	T	W	T	F	S
1	2	3	4	5	6	7
8	9	10	11	12	13	14
15	16	17	18	19	20	21
22	23	24	25	26	27	28
29	30	31				

February 12 is Abraham Lincoln's birthday.
In 2006, what day of the week is his birthday?
Use the calendar to help you.

Suppose you can't see a clock or a watch.
How could you tell about what time of day it is?
Compare your ideas with a friend's ideas.

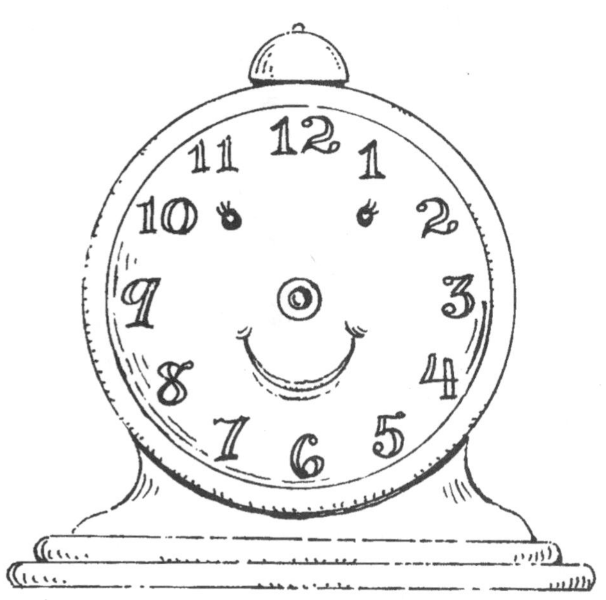

© Dale Seymour Publications®

Fill in the blanks in the story.

The story must make sense.

Jamie has _______ quarters.

Vera has _______ dimes.

Tamika has _______ nickels.

They each have the same amount of money.

Altogether, they have _______.

Compare your story with a friend's story.

Two bags together hold $12.

Bag A holds twice as much money as bag B.

How much money is in each bag?

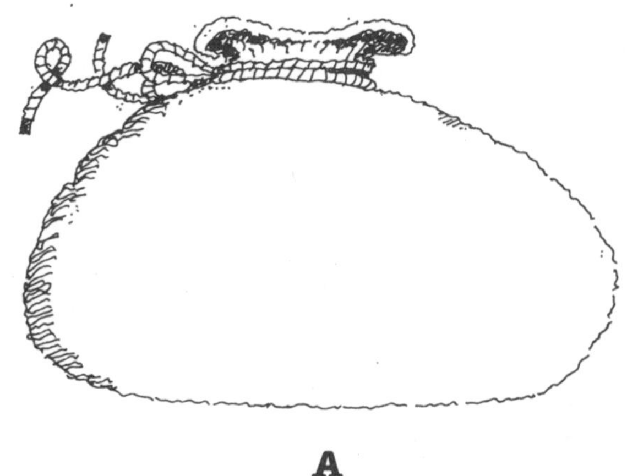

A

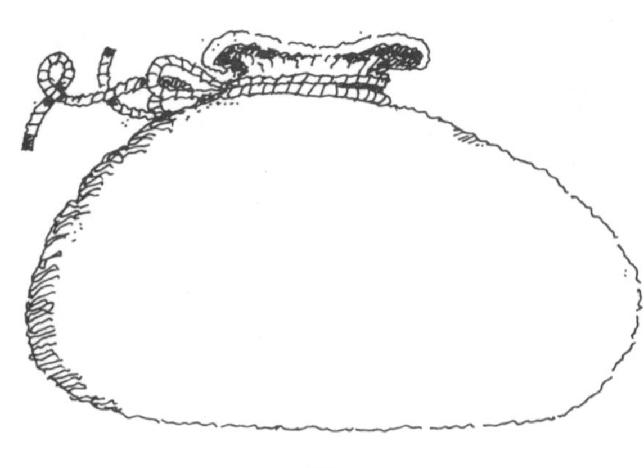

B

This clock is 20 minutes slow.

Show the correct time on this clock.

This clock is 20 minutes fast.

Show the correct time on this clock.

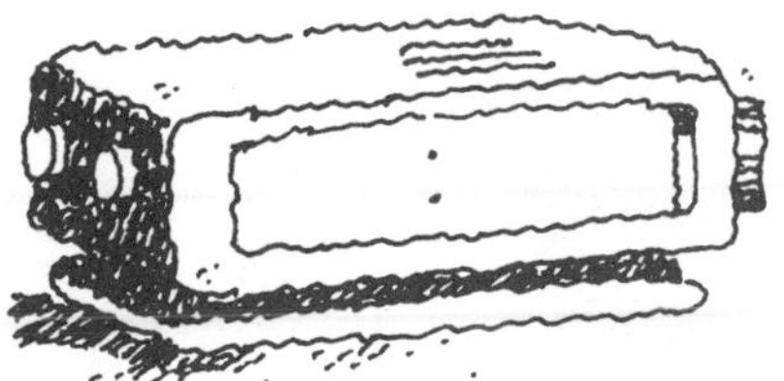

Who had more sleep, Nigel or Theo?

How many more minutes?

Tell how you decided.

Check your answer with a friend's answer.

Did you solve the problem the same way?

© Dale Seymour Publications®

45

Here is a way to compare dog ages to people ages.

Rule
dog years × 7 = people years

Fido was born 8 years ago.

Spot is 42 "people years" old.

- Which dog is older, Fido or Spot?
- By how many dog years?
- By how many people years?

46

Which season is the favorite?

Ask 10 people you know in your neighborhood.

Compare your data with data your classmates collect.

Baseball Cards
3 different brands
20¢ each

You have 3 quarters and 4 dimes.

How many baseball cards can you buy?

Tell two ways to decide.

I have $13 to spend on my vacation.

I have 2 bills and 4 coins.

What are the bills and coins?

BILL

2 sandwiches

1 glass of lemonade

Total: $5.40

BILL

1 sandwich

1 glass of lemonade

Total: $3.45

Use these stamps.

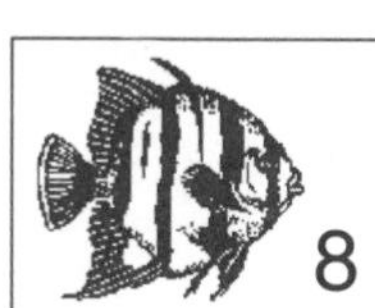

What is the fewest number of stamps you need to make exactly $1 in postage?

What stamps did you use?

Can you do it another way? How?

© Dale Seymour Publications®

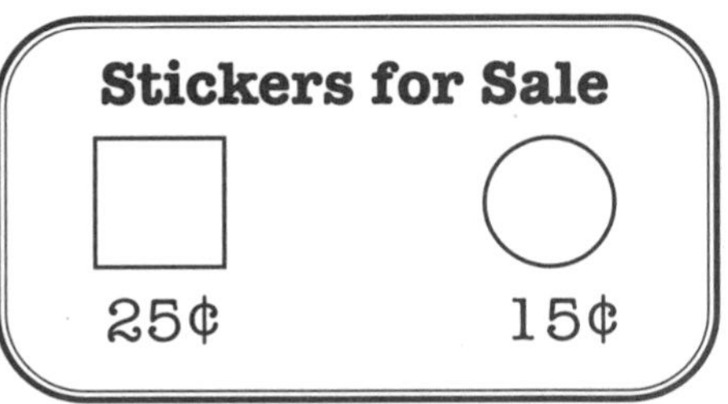

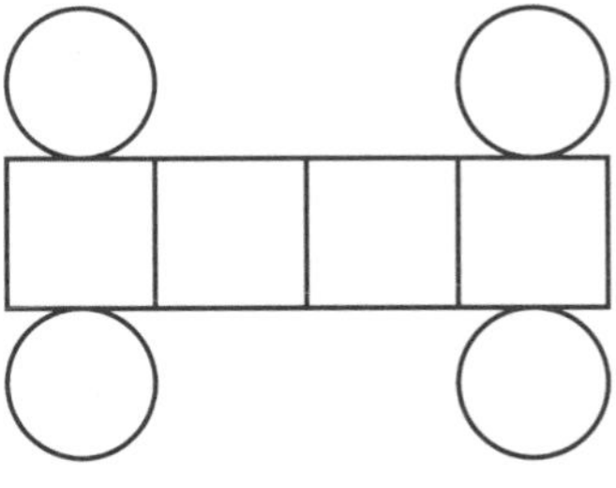

Picture A

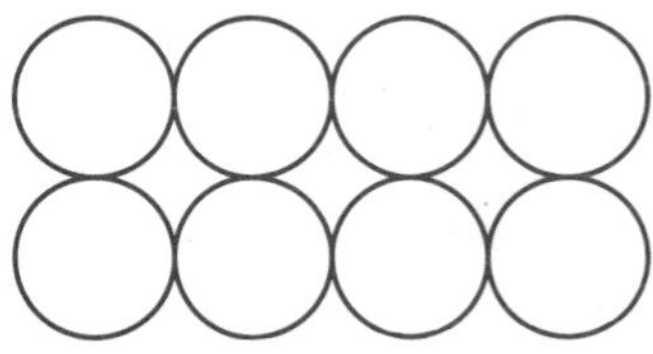

Picture B

How much more does picture A cost than picture B?

Tell two ways to decide.

Sam has some money.

- He spends 39¢.
- He earns $2.00 delivering a package.
- Now he has $3.10.

How much money did Sam have in the beginning?

53

What coins are in the dolphin bank?

- The bank has 48¢.
- There are 14 coins.
- There are half as many nickels as pennies.
- There are half as many dimes as nickels.

There are _____ pennies, _____ nickels, and _____ dimes.

For the year 2000, the United States decided to mint a different quarter to honor each state.

If you collect a complete set, how much money will you have?

© Dale Seymour Publications®

Use the clues to identify the owner of each bank.

Write the names on the lines.

It takes about 2 minutes to

______________________________.

It takes about 3 hours to

______________________________.

It takes about 5 days to

______________________________.

Fill in each blank with an activity that makes sense.

Ask 10 kids when they ate dinner last night.

Record the times on a list.

- What is the earliest time?
- What is the latest time?
- What is the most common time?
- How many minutes from the earliest time to the latest time?

58

You have a vacation day to plan.

Write at least 6 activities you will do that day.

Make a schedule.

Tell what time each activity starts and ends.

Tell how long you will spend doing each activity.

59

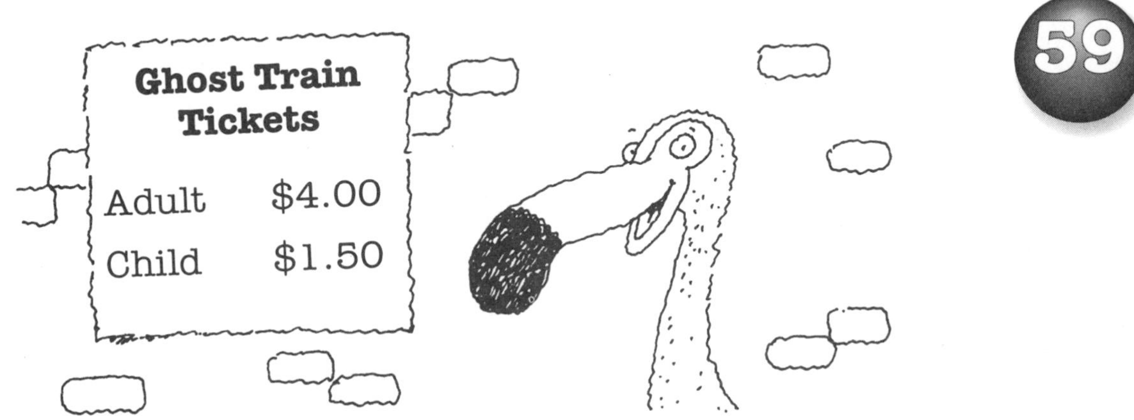

The Mayos rode on the Ghost Train.

The tickets cost $12.50 altogether.

How many Mayo children went on the Ghost Train?

Tell how you know.

60

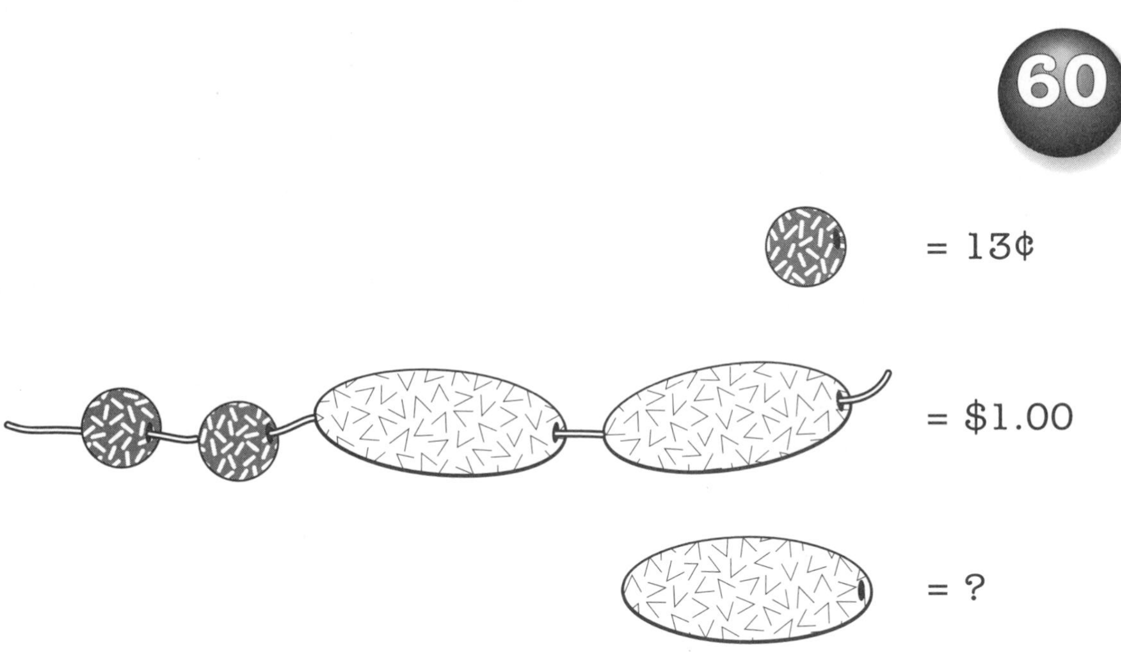

61

Use the numbers on the train cars.

Put a number in each blank.

The story must make sense.

Carla got on the train at ______.

After ______ minutes, or at ______, she arrived at her stop.

She shopped for ______ hours.

She returned to the train station at ______.

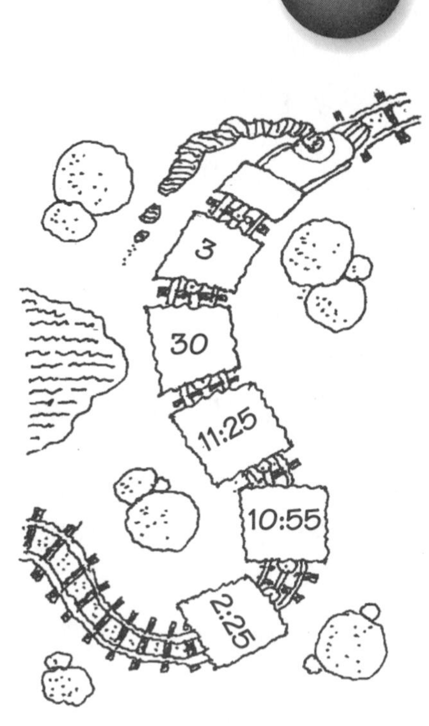

62

April 10

November 10

June 29

March 17

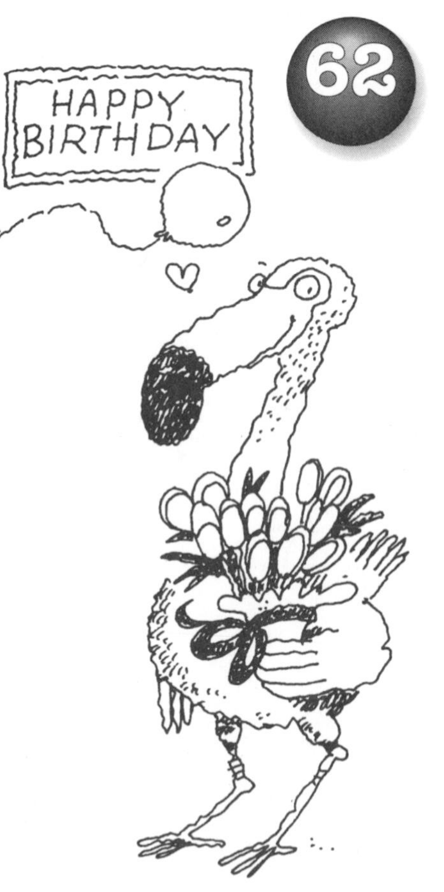

Talia's birthday is one of these dates.

- It is not in the same month as Thanksgiving.
- The month has 30 days.
- It is not in the summer.

Which date is her birthday?

You have $31.

How many more car washes can you get with the special than by paying the regular price?

64

You have $1.15 to spend at the yard sale.

You don't want to buy more than one of any item.

Find 3 ways to spend all of your money.

65

Tyrone bought turtle stamps.

Tom bought moose stamps.

They spent the same amount of money.

Who got more stamps?

Tell how you know.

Look at this square tile.

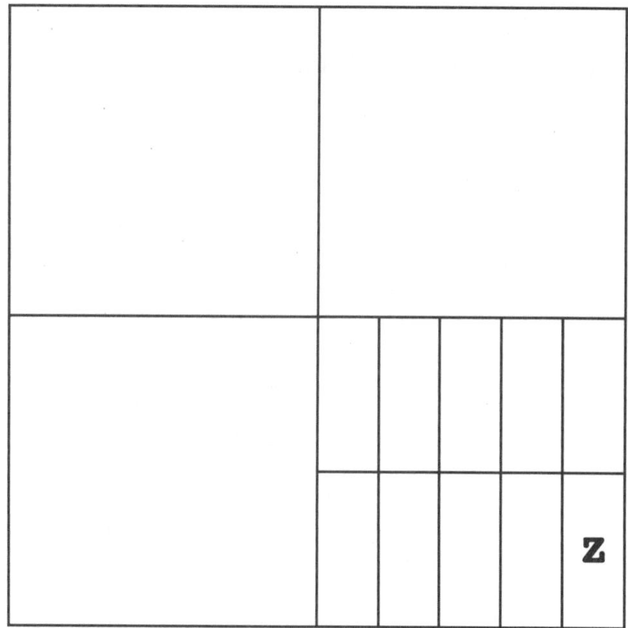

The square tile is $4.00. How much does Z cost?

© Dale Seymour Publications®

Make a rectangle around 4 numbers in the month.

Add the 2 numbers on each diagonal.

Do this for 3 other rectangles of 4 numbers.

What do you notice?

Why do you think this happens?

October

S	M	T	W	T	F	S
				1	2	3
4	5	6	7	8	9	10
11	12	13	14	15	16	17
18	19	20	21	22	23	24
25	26	27	28	29	30	31

It is Wednesday, December 28.

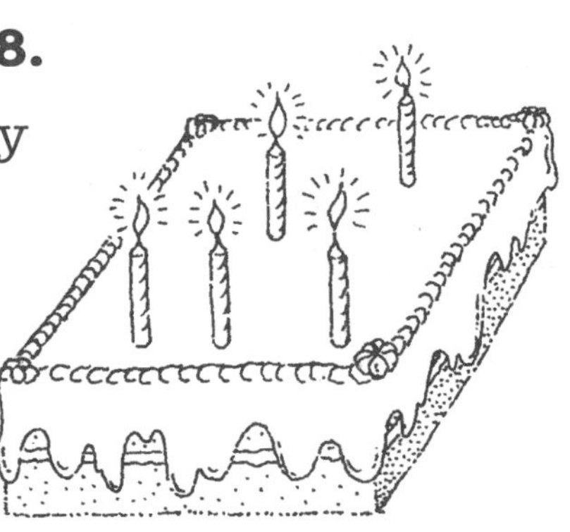

- Palani's birthday is exactly 2 weeks from today.
- Kyle's birthday is in 18 days.
- Daniel's birthday is on January 12.

Whose birthday is first? On what date? On which day of the week?

Whose birthday is last? On what date? On which day of the week?

© Dale Seymour Publications®

69

Opal bought a magazine and 3 newspapers.

She spent $3.75 in all.

The magazine cost $2.25.

The price of each newspaper was the same.

How much did each newspaper cost?

70

You have:

You want to buy 1 sticker using exact change.

You can buy a 36¢ sticker. How?

You cannot buy a 24¢ sticker. Why not?

What different-value stickers can you buy with exact change? List them all.

© Dale Seymour Publications®

Gia and Brandon have the same amount of money.

Gia has 4 coins that are alike.

Brandon has 3 coins that are all different.

How much money do they each have?

Bagel Special!

Buy 1 for 50¢.

Get the second for 15¢.

Mr. Spencer spent $1.30 for bagels.

How many bagels did he buy?

Arnon bought 3 different items and spent $3.65.

What did Arnon buy?

Find another answer.

pencils 65¢ each

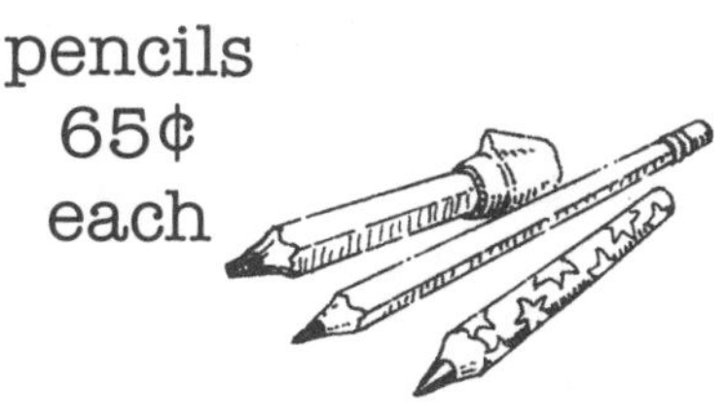

paste $1.05

milk 35¢

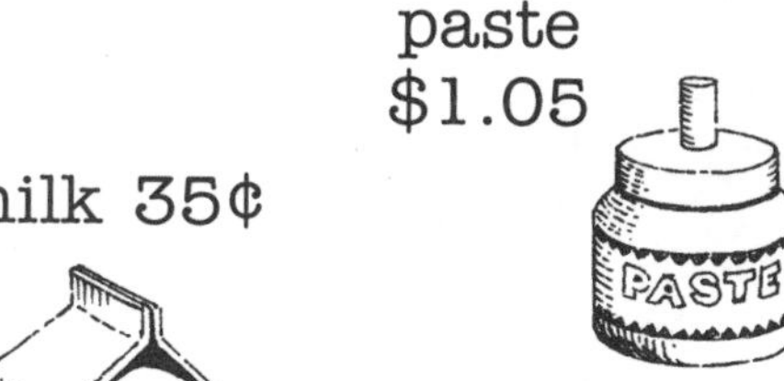

disks 75¢ each

stapler $2.25

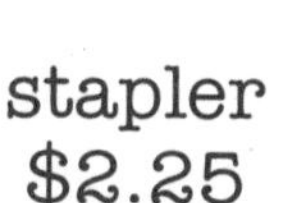

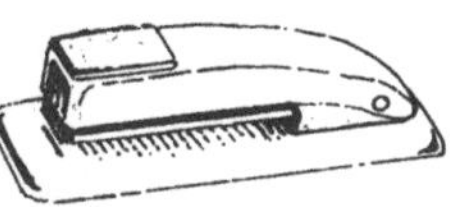

74

Russ has $4 more than Milo.

Together, they have $26.

How much money does Russ have?

Tell how you know.

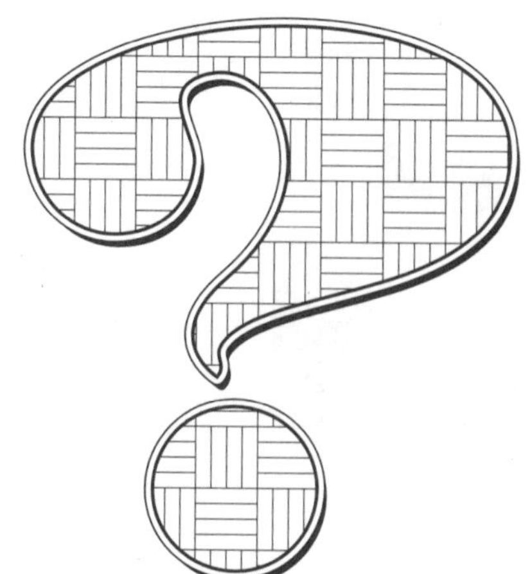

© Dale Seymour Publications®

It is 11:30 A.M.

Maddy has a golf lesson in 45 minutes.

She goes to lunch after her half-hour lesson.

At what time does Maddy go to lunch?

76

Think of a digital clock.

Name all of the times when the digits add to 20.

4 + 5 + 2 = 11

4:52

© Dale Seymour Publications®

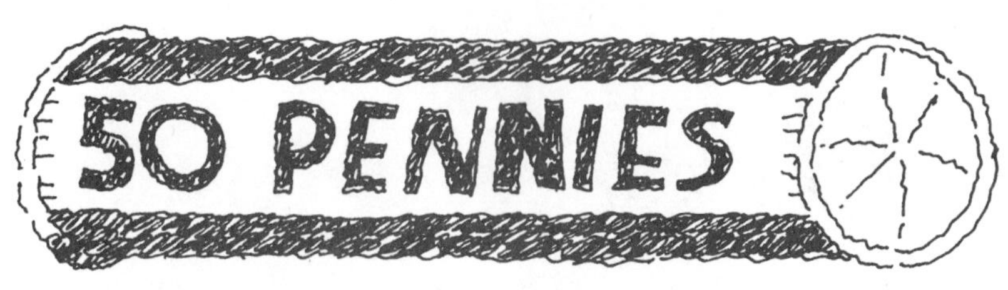

Isaac has 4 rolls of pennies.

Sara has 1 roll of dimes.

How many dimes should Sara give to Isaac so they have the same amount of money?

List the steps you used to find the answer.

78

Make a "quarter flower."

- Put one quarter down. It will be the center.
- Use more quarters to make a ring of "petals" around the center.

How many quarters are in your flower?

How much money is that?

Now make a "nickel flower."

How much money is a nickel flower worth?

How much more is a quarter flower worth than a nickel flower?

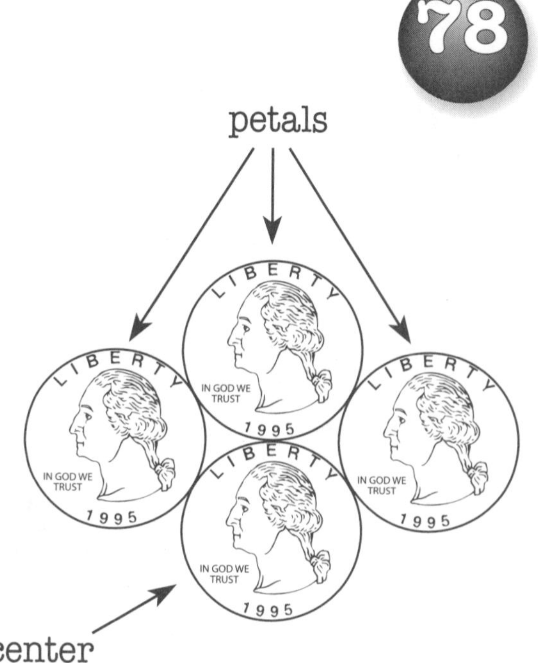

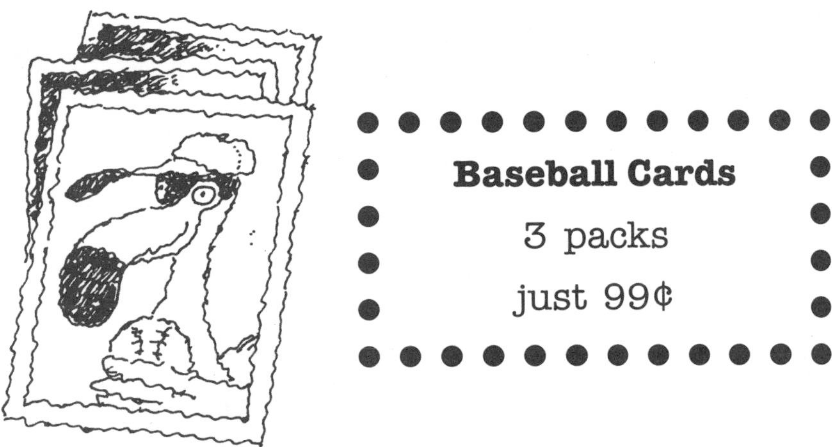

What is the price of a dozen packs of cards?

Tell two ways to decide.

80

I bought 3 different items.

I paid with a $10 bill.

I got $1.51 in change.

What did I buy?

81

The dance marathon started on Tuesday at 9 A.M.

It ended 36 hours later.

What day did the marathon end?

What time did the marathon end?

82

I parked from 9:05 in the morning to
1:30 in the afternoon.

How much did I pay for parking?

The distance across a quarter, its *diameter*, is about 1 inch.

Imagine a line of quarters as tall as you.

How much money is that?

Use a calculator to help you.

Compare your answer with the answers of some friends.

Fill in the TV schedule.

- The *movie* is 90 minutes long.
- The *music video* show is 45 minutes long.
- The *exercise* show begins right after the 5-minute *movie review*.
- The *mystery* is 30 minutes long.
- The *morning news* is 15 minutes long.

Time	Program
8:00	
8:15	talk show
8:45	
9:30	
10:00	
10:05	
11:00	
12:30	cartoon

85

1 HOUR 100 MINUTES 1000 SECONDS

86

The Lawsons went on a hike.

They left at 7:30 in the morning,
walked for 1 hour 15 minutes,
rested for 10 minutes,
walked for another 70 minutes,
and then stopped for breakfast.

At what time did they stop for breakfast?

You want to buy some Nut Crunchy peanut butter.

Should you shop at Pepe's or Craig's?

Explain.

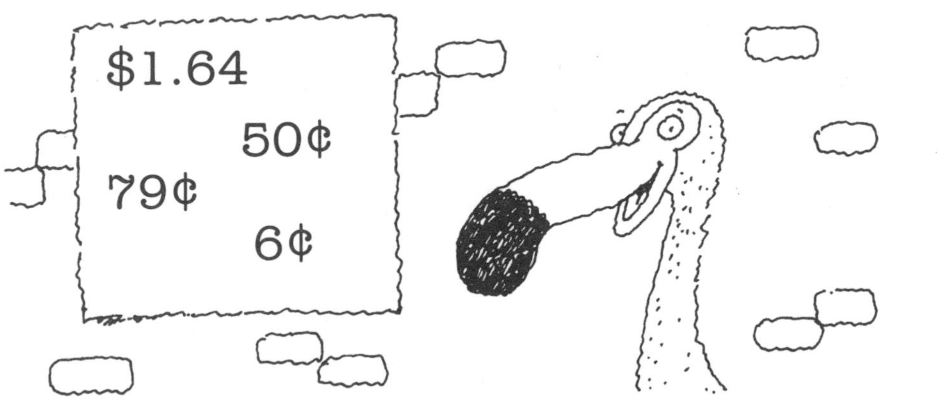

88

Use the facts.

Write four questions.

The answers must be on the sign.

Facts

- Caspian has 6 dimes and 1 quarter.
- Kathy has 3 quarters and 4 pennies.

The race started at 11:00 A.M.

The winner crossed the finish line at 1:28 P.M.

The last runner crossed the finish line at 2:10 P.M.

How many more minutes did it take the last runner to finish than the winner?

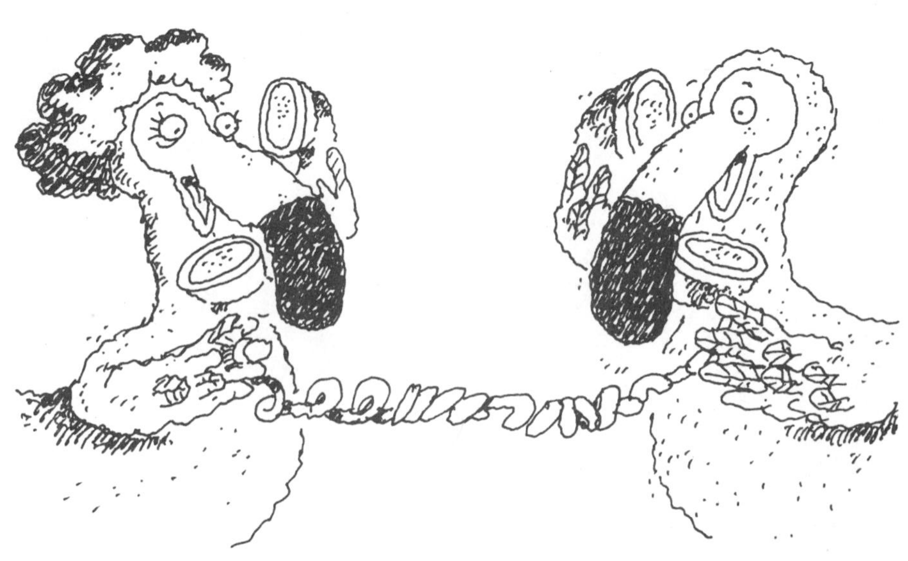

Shikara called her mother at 7:41 at night.

The call ended at 8:12 at night.

At 5¢ per minute, how much did the call cost?

91

What is the price of 10 stickers?

Tell two ways to decide.

= $1.50

= $.90

= ?

© Dale Seymour Publications®

Ned: "Hurry up! It's only 30 minutes until the magic show."

Jason: "Take your time. It's many hours until the magic show."

Why do you think Ned and Jason disagree? Explain.

MAGIC SHOW

8:00

94

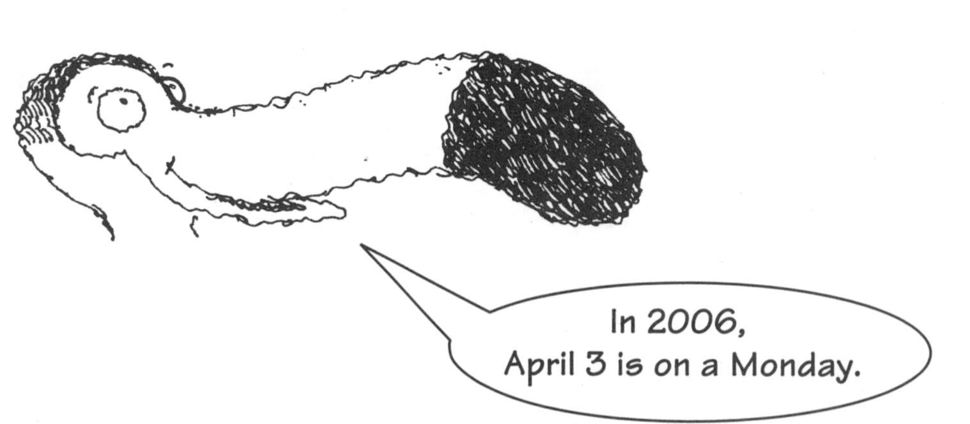

How many Mondays are in April 2006?

Tell how you know.

Today is Tuesday, May 15.

Our vacation begins on Tuesday, June 19.

How many weeks until our vacation begins?

Write the correct birth date for each child.

Order the children from youngest to oldest.

97

You want the most money.

Would you rather have a dollar for the number of

- days in October or days in April?
- years in a decade or months in a year?
- days in a year or seconds in 10 minutes?

pear + grapes + apple = 95¢

pear + apple = 55¢

© Dale Seymour Publications®

Which store has the better buy?

How did you decide?

I put 4 quarters in the parking meter.

How many minutes can I park?

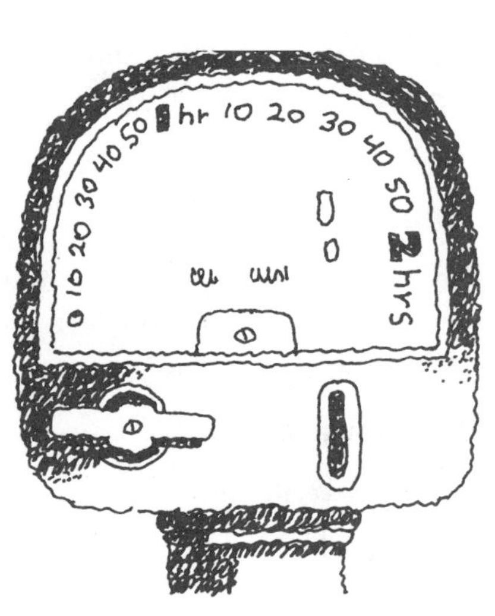

Answers

1. *The Toy Robot,* 25 min longer; Possible explanation: 1 h 10 min is 70 min, which is 25 min less than 95 min.
2. 1:35
3. Kai, Will, Tess
4. skates and shoes
5. Story problems will vary.
6. July
7. 21¢
8. \$15, \$18, \$11
9. 30¢, 35¢, 48¢, 39¢
10. Answers will vary.
11. 7:03
12. 2:53; Explanations will vary.
13. \$1.50
14. Math problems will vary.
15. 10 seconds, 2 hours, 8 months; Questions will vary.
16. Feb 10, Oct 17, Mar 25
17. 5 dimes; Explanations will vary.
18. 67 h
19. Answers will vary.
20. \$24 more; Possible explanation: The grade 4 students sold $7 \times 4 = 28$ boxes while the grade 3 students sold $4 \times 4 = 16$ boxes, which is $28 - 16 = 12$ boxes more, or $12 \times \$2 = \$24$ more.
21. \$6.50 (one \$5 bill and 3 half dollars); Explanations will vary.
22. Stories will vary.
23. 7: 2 half dollars, 1 quarter, 1 dime, 3 pennies; 138: 138 pennies
24. \$1.75; Possible explanations: $12 - 5 = 7$, and 7 quarters is \$1.75. *Or,* 12 quarters is \$3.00 and 5 quarters is \$1.25, and $\$3.00 - \$1.25 = \$1.75$.
25. \$3.60
26. \$1.25 more
27. yes; Possible explanation: If you round to $80 + 110 + 80 + 60$ it equals \$3.30, and you have increased, more than decreased, the prices.
28. 1 penny, 1 dime, 1 quarter
29. \$3.30 more
30. \$1.30
31. $7\frac{1}{2}$ h *or* 7 h 30 min
32. 7:35 P.M.
33. 6 pennies, 2 quarters, 2 dimes
34. \$22.40
35. \$2.50; Explanations will vary.
36. \$1.31
37. a dime for each week of the year; Explanations will vary.
38. 2052, 300, 1752, 1776
39. Sunday
40. Possible answers: location of the sun, length of shadows, length of time awake, what people are doing
41. Stories will vary.
42. A has \$8; B has \$4.
43. 12:05, 1:53
44. Theo, 5 more min; Solution methods will vary.
45. Fido, 2 dog years, 14 people years

46. Answers will vary.
47. 5 cards; Possible explanations: 3 quarters + 4 dimes = $1.15, and you can buy 5 cards for $1.00 and no more for the leftover 15¢. *Or,* 3 quarters will buy 3 cards, and 4 dimes will buy 2 cards, leaving 15¢ change.
48. $1 bill, $10 bill, 4 half dollars
49. $1.95
50. 11 stamps; Any two of the following ways: eight 11¢ stamps, one 8¢ stamp, two 2¢ stamps *or* seven 11¢ stamps, two 8¢ stamps, one 5¢ stamp, one 2¢ stamp *or* six 11¢ stamps, three 8¢ stamps, two 5¢ stamps *or* five 11¢ stamps, five 8¢ stamps, one 5¢ stamp *or* four 11¢ stamps, seven 8¢ stamps
51. 40¢ more; Possible explanations: 4 circles are 60¢ and 4 squares are $1.00, totaling $1.60; 8 circles are $1.20; and $1.60 – $1.20 = 40¢. *Or,* eliminate 4 circles from each picture; 4 squares are $1.00 and 4 circles are $.60, and $1.00 – $.60 = $.40.
52. $1.49
53. 8, 4, 2
54. $12.50
55. Kim Su, $1.25; Lucy, 79¢; Karem, $2.18; Taylor, $1.58
56. Answers will vary.
57. Answers will vary.
58. Answers will vary.
59. 3 children; Explanations will vary.
60. 37¢
61. 10:55, 30, 11:25, 3, 2:25
62. April 10
63. 2 more
64. There are 4 ways: doll, toy truck *or* doll, ball, book *or* puzzle, toy truck, book *or* toy truck, ball, book, cap
65. Tyrone; Explanations will vary.
66. 10¢
67. The diagonal sums are equal. Explanations will vary.
68. Palani, Jan 11, Wed; Kyle, Jan 15, Sun
69. 50¢
70. For a 36¢ sticker, use 1 quarter, 1 dime, and 1 penny. You can't make exactly 24¢ with this set of coins. You can buy a sticker with a value of 1¢, 5¢, 6¢, 10¢, 11¢, 15¢, 16¢, 20¢, 21¢, 25¢, 26¢, 30¢, 31¢, 35¢, 36¢, 40¢, 41¢, 45¢, or 46¢.
71. 40¢
72. 4 bagels
73. stapler, paste, milk *or* stapler, pencil, disk
74. $15; Explanations will vary.
75. 12:45 P.M.
76. 6:59, 7:58, 7:49, 8:57, 8:48, 8:39, 9:56, 9:47, 9:38, 9:29
77. 10 dimes; Possible steps: Sara has $4. Isaac has $2. Sara has to give $1 to Isaac so they both have $3.
78. 7 quarters (the center and 6 petals); $1.75; $.35; A quarter flower is worth $1.40 more than a nickel flower.
79. $3.96; Possible explanations: One pack is 99¢ ÷ 3 = 33¢, so 12 packs are 12 × 33¢ = $3.96. *Or,* a dozen packs is 4 × 3, so the price of a dozen packs is 4 × 99¢ = $3.96.
80. ball, jump rope, balloon
81. Wed, 9 P.M.
82. $7.50
83. Answers will vary.

84. morning news, talk show, music video, mystery, movie review, exercise, movie, cartoon
85. 100 min
86. 10:05 in the morning
87. Craig's Market has the better buy, but if you want only 8 oz, you should buy at Pepe's Tienda (assuming Craig's doesn't carry a smaller size).
88. Possible answer: How much money do they have together? ($1.64) How much more money does Caspian have than Kathy? (6¢) How much money does Kathy have? (79¢) How much more money does Kathy have in quarters than Caspian has in quarters? (50¢)
89. 42 min more
90. $1.55
91. $1.00; Possible explanations: 5 is $\frac{1}{3}$ of 15, and $\frac{1}{3}$ of $1.50 is 50¢, so 5 stickers cost 50¢ and 10 stickers cost 2 × 50¢ = $1.00. *Or,* 1 sticker costs $1.50 ÷ 15 = 10¢, so 10 stickers cost 10 × 10¢ = $1.00.
92. $1.20
93. Possible answer: It's 7:30 A.M.; Ned thinks the show is at 8:00 A.M. and Jason thinks it's at 8:00 P.M.
94. 4 Mondays; Explanations will vary.
95. 5 weeks
96. From youngest to oldest: Pedro: Aug 15, 1992; Tanya: Jul 15, 1991; Kiki: Jul 1, 1991; Margo: Aug 1, 1990
97. days in October, months in a year, seconds in 10 minutes
98. 80¢
99. Design Store; Possible explanation: 1 yd = 36 in., and 18 in. is half a yard, and half the price at the Design Store is about 63¢, which is less than the price at the Party Store.
100. 30 min